UNFOLDING HER

The Sacred Becoming of a Woman Remembered

By

Francesca Tonge

*For the woman I was,
for the woman I am,
and for the woman I am still becoming.*

*For the sister circle who held my name
when I nearly forgot it myself—
your love has been both mirror and medicine.*

*For every woman
who has ever lost herself
in love,
in work,
in longing,
and found her way home again.*

*For you.
For us.
For the unfolding.*

This book was as organic as it was intentional.

*I didn't set out to write a book.
For years, my poems were personal—
journal entries, private prayers,
little pieces of myself rarely offered to the world.*

*But in the process of my own healing,
my own rebirth,
I began to realize:
these pages weren't meant for me alone.*

*What I had written to survive,
to unearth,
to reclaim,
could be medicine for other women
and even a glimpse into womanhood for men
willing to witness.*

*This book grew from need—
my own,
and the universal ache of all women
who have ever questioned their worth,
buried their softness,
or doubted the power of their own becoming.*

*May these pages remind you:
you were never alone,
and you were never broken.
You have simply been...
unfolding.*

Sections

- *Remembering Her*
- *Reclaiming Her*
- *Revealing Her*
- *Unapologetically Unbothered*
- *The Becoming After the Believing*
- *In the Presence of Real Love*
- *What She Walked Away From*

Remembering Her

__Thanks for Fumbling Me__

To the one who met me
when my spirit still wore my grandmother's plaits,
thank you for making me believe
love was play,
before I learned
that even playgrounds
can turn to battlegrounds.
You fumbled —
but it's cool.
You taught me
that sweetness alone
doesn't hold a woman.

To the one whose laughter
felt like sunlight,
whose hands
let go too soon,
thank you for showing me
that even joy
can slip through careless fingers.
You fumbled —
but that's alright.
You reminded me
that I am worthy
of being chosen,
not just entertained.

To the one who wore a ring
but never wore the weight
of partnership,

thank you for breaking
what was never whole.
You fumbled —
and I bless you.
Because in your absence,
I filled my own name
with meaning.

To the ones
who came wrapped in lessons,
who mistook me for a landing
when I was meant to soar,
thank you.
Each stumble,
each silence,
each betrayal
pushed me closer
to the door I was always meant to open.

And now—
I walk into a love
where I do not need to shrink,
where I do not have to beg,
where the fumble
was the fire
that forged me.

So yes—
thank you.
Because without your empty hands,
mine would have never learned
how to be full.

Sip From Her Own Glass

She used to wait,
cup in hand,
for someone
to fill her.

A drop of attention here,
a splash of affection there —
thirsty for love
poured from someone else's bottle.

But now—
she sips from her own glass.

She toasts the mirror,
drinks in her reflection,
lets the taste of her own worth
linger on her tongue.

She learned
that no hand
could steady her
like her own.

That no mouth
could quench her
like the words
she speaks to herself
in the quiet.

She is no longer parched
for validation.
She's drunk
on her own becoming,

savored in small sips,
never needing
to beg for a pour.

Wake Up to Your Truth

Can't do it.
Won't attempt.
I'm stuck—
or stubborn.

It's comfortable here.
It shouldn't be.
It should tear me apart.
Why doesn't it?

Am I normal?
Hell no.
Do I want to be?
Not anymore.

Confusion was the drug.
Circling the same ache
like it was holy.
Worshipping the wound
instead of healing it.

I called it mystery.
I called it edge.
But truth?
It was fear.

Plain, sharp,
unromantic fear.
Fear of power.
Of desire.
Of the fire
that would burn
the old versions of me
to ash.

Terrified not of the fall—
but of the rise.
Because rising means
no more hiding.
No more waiting.
No more performing
smallness for applause.

I was designed
to break out,
not break down.

And now?
I will not shrink.
I will not apologize.
I will not carry
the weight of people
who never learned
to carry themselves.

I am awake.
Blazing.
Unbothered.
Unfolding
into everything
they told me to fear.

Let them call it too much.
Let them call it wild.
Let them call it selfish.
I call it:
finally mine.

Loneliness Was Never Meant to Break Me

There were nights
loneliness wrapped itself around me
like a second skin.
Nights when silence wasn't peace—
it was punishment.
Nights when the only person
who ever called me beautiful
was the woman who birthed me,
and I wondered if she said it
because she had to,
not because it was true.

There were men who saw my body,
but never my soul.
Men who begged for pieces of me,
then tossed loose change at my worth
like I was something borrowed,
something bought.
Men who promised love,
but packed their loyalty
in carry-on bags
they never intended to unpack.

Then came the day
love didn't leave—
it revealed.
Revealed the part of me
still willing to shrink
for a seat at someone else's table.
Revealed the ache that thought
I had to earn
what should have been given.

I sank into loneliness so deep,
it felt like drowning.
Lonely for arms that didn't exist,
lonely for babies
my body wouldn't carry,
lonely for a family
that wasn't mine to hold.

Inside that loneliness,
my body still craved the touch
of the unworthy—
just to feel something
other than the hollow weight of solitude.

I lied to myself,
said I could move like them.
Said I could treat men like they treated me:
use them,
discard them,
never feel a thing.

And for a moment, it worked.
For a moment, I wore hardness like armor,
mistook numbness for power.

But I wasn't built for that kind of violence
against my own spirit.

My softness broke through every time.
No matter how hard I tried to pretend,
I couldn't erase the tenderness
written into my bones.
I couldn't be cold.
I couldn't stay untouched.

And so again,
I was left open—
vulnerable to their disrespect,
their fake love,
their hollow promises
that never knew how to hold
the weight of a real woman.

But loneliness—
loneliness wasn't sent to break me.
It was sent to rebuild me.

Because in the ashes
of what I thought I needed,
I started sweeping my own floors.
Lighting my own candles.
Speaking life into friends
who, like me,
had mistaken survival for living.

I built altars out of laughter.
I carved joy into quiet mornings.
I poured love into every crack
they said was too wide to fill.

And somewhere in the tending—
I bloomed.

Not because someone loved me.
Not because someone stayed.
But because I stayed.
I stayed for myself.

Now I know:

I am not half of a whole.
I am not waiting to be chosen.
I am not a hunger waiting to be fed.

I am whole
all by my damn self.

And love—
real love—
is not a life raft.
It is a blessing
to a woman
who already learned how to swim.

So yes, I still desire love.
I still crave connection.
But it will never again
be the engine of my becoming.

I savor the love I have.
I pour into myself
until the overflow
attracts only what's worthy.

Because loneliness taught me:
I was never empty.
I was just waiting
to remember
how full I already was.

Reclaiming Her

Becoming

I am not who I was,
and I am nowhere near finished.

I am the woman
who walked through fire
and learned to love the smell of smoke.
The one who buried old versions of herself
and grew wildflowers from the graves.

I am the soft after the storm,
the calm that learned
how to roar when necessary,
the peace that knows its own weight.

I used to wonder
if I was too much,
if my light was too bright,
if my heart was too wide open.

Now I know:
I was only ever too much
for those who were never enough.

I have traded apology for power,
self-doubt for self-devotion,
and scarcity for a love
that overflows in every direction.

I have become the thing
I was once waiting for—
the rescue,
the remedy,
the revolution.

This is not arrival.
This is becoming.
And every day,
I unfold a little more
into the woman
I was always meant to be.

She's the Flame and the Feast

She is radiant,
not because the world gave her light,
but because she lit the match herself.
She is the fire and the food it warms—
the feast,
the prayer,
and the hand that serves it.

She speaks in layers,
moves in truth,
and loves in metaphor.
A touch from her feels like poetry,
even when she's saying nothing at all.

She's the woman you pray for
and the storm you call down.
Soft hands, sharp mind,
a giver with boundaries that only love should dare test.
She's not meant for halves,
and she'll never be held by hands
that don't know how to honor the whole.

Her intuition is divine—
she sees you
even when you've hidden from yourself.
But don't mistake her kindness for confusion.
She may love you past reason,
but she will walk away with every ounce of her dignity
if you teach her how to leave.

She's romantic, but not naive.
She's fallen before,
but never without wings.
Now she loves differently—

strategically, spiritually,
like a goddess who's learned that to be chosen
starts with choosing herself.

She's been the partner,
the parent,
the provider,
the peace.
She's poured from empty
and still made it taste like wine.

Now she sips from her own glass—
finally.
And it's sweet.

She's no longer explaining her worth,
auditioning for affection,
shrinking to be softer.
She's expanding, glowing,
demanding full presence or nothing at all.

And you—if you're lucky—
you'll witness it.

You'll see a woman
who is the whole sky and the storm,
the hand and the harvest,
the echo and the origin.

She's the flame and the feast.

And if you can't love her right,
at least love her from a distance—
because up close,
she's unforgettable.

Anyway

I loved anyway.
After the breaking,
after the bitter,
after the silence carved into bone—
I still opened my hands.
Still opened my heart.
Still said yes
to the trembling risk
of something new.

I loved anyway,
even when the mirror
showed me cracks
where innocence once lived,
even when I was sure
my softness had been spent.

I loved anyway—
because that's who I am.
Because somewhere beneath the scar tissue,
beneath the ache,
beneath the memory of doors slammed and voices raised,
I knew:
love was never the enemy.

It was the choosing of the unready.
It was the begging of the unwilling.
It was the mistaking of attention
for devotion.

But me?
I was built to love
in spite of.
Because of.

Through.
Beyond.

I loved anyway,
and that became my alchemy.
Not the pain,
but the rising after.

Not the loss,
but the way I stayed soft
when the world told me to harden.

I loved anyway—
and in the end,
that love folded back into me,
wrapped me in grace,
and whispered:
you are already everything
you were waiting for.

This Peace Ain't Free

Once upon a time,
access to me was easy.
My laughter, my softness, my sparkle—
given freely,
like breath.
Like grace.

But growth charges interest.
And this peace?
This piece?
This sacred slice of me?
It ain't free anymore.

Friendships that fed on chaos—
gone.
Lovers who dined on convenience—
starved.
Conversations that drained instead of nourished—
canceled mid-sentence.

I am not a free sample.
I am not a flash sale.
I am not a "once you get bored, toss it aside" clearance rack prize.

This peace?
It costs intentionality.
It costs truth-telling.
It costs healed hands, soft words, and presence that feels like prayer.

You want this piece of me?
You want a seat at my table?
You better come with energy that pays full price,

plus tax,
plus tip,
plus tithes to the goddess within me.

Because dusty energy can't afford the new rates.
Manipulators can't finesse the new currency.
Half-effort love can't purchase full access.

If your spirit ain't rich,
your wallet ain't heavy enough.
If your respect ain't deep,
your hands ain't clean enough.

So yeah—
the price inflated.
The gates lifted.
The standard rose.

Because this peace?
This piece?
This sacred woman I became?
She ain't free.
Not anymore.

Somebody's Treasure

Before they praised me,
before they pursued me,
before they even knew my name—
I was already somebody's treasure.

Before the heartbreaks tried to shrink me,
before the loneliness tried to empty me,
before the world tried to weigh me against lesser things—
I was already enough.

Already precious.
Already whole.
Already sacred.

It took me years to stop auditioning for worthiness.
To stop handing out pieces of myself
in hopes that someone would call them gold.

It took the right voice,
the right love,
the right moment—
to whisper what I should have always known:

"You were never waiting to be chosen.
You were never broken.
You were never invisible."

I was somebody's treasure
long before they recognized the gleam.
Long before they saw the way I could light up a room
or resurrect a dying dream.

And now,
I don't need them to find me valuable
to know that I am.

Now,
I polish my own shine.
Now,
I cradle my own worth.
Now,
I live like the masterpiece
I was always destined to be.

I am not looking for a place to belong.
I *am* the belonging.
I *am* the blessing.
I *am* the treasure I was waiting for.

Agent of Chaos

I call myself an agent of chaos—
but not the kind you fear.
Not the chaos that breaks things
just to hear the sound.

I am the chaos
that drags truth into the light,
that pries open locked drawers
where pain has been hoarded.

I believe in upheaval.
In the holy mess of healing.
I will not let shadows grow roots
where love should live.

You can't heal
what you hide.
You can't call it peace
if it's built on silence
and swallowed screams.

So I tear it open.
I pull the grief out by its roots.
I name the ache.
I name the wound.
I name the longing
that pretends it's anger.

And yes,
it gets loud.
It gets messy.
It gets uncomfortable
before it gets clean.

But I was never made
to sit quiet in the corner
while the house burned down.

I was made to walk into the fire,
to pull out the pieces worth saving,
and set the rest aflame.

Let them call me too much.
Let them call me destructive.
I call it sacred demolition.

Because after the collapse
comes the rising.

And I will always
be willing
to rise.

Revealing Her

She Loves Herself First

She learned,
finally,
to love herself first.

Not in the hashtag,
bubble bath,
sip-and-selfie way—
but in the quiet,
unyielding,
sacred way.

In the way she said no
without guilt.
In the way she fed her body
good food
and her soul
better company.

In the way she stopped
waiting for apologies
that never came,
and gave herself
the closure
she deserved.

She loves herself first
by unlearning the art
of overgiving.
By untangling her worth
from the hands
that never learned
how to hold her.

She learned to listen
to the girl inside—
the one she ignored
for years.
She asked her,
"What do you need, baby?"
And this time,
she listened.

She loves herself first
because she knows
love that demands
her absence
from herself
is not love at all.

She loves herself first
because she knows
that when love comes,
the right kind,
it will only add
to the fire
she already lit
within.

And now,
anyone who enters her life
must know—
this heart,
this body,
this brilliant, soft, wild woman—
is already spoken for.

By her.
First.
And always.

Holy Ground

This body—
my body—
is holy ground.

Not because anyone said so,
not because anyone touched it right,
but because I
have finally remembered it.

These thighs,
these arms,
this belly soft with survival,
this skin kissed by sun and story—
they hold the map
of every place I've walked through
and every place I refused to stay.

There was a time
when I handed myself over
like an offering,
hoping to be worshipped,
only to be wounded.
A time when I mistook
desire for devotion,
attention for affection,
touch for truth.

But not anymore.

Now,
I smooth lotion into my skin
like an invocation.
I dance in the mirror
with no one watching,

and call it ceremony.
I speak to myself kindly
and call it prayer.

I am not waiting
for someone to arrive
and name me worthy.
I was already carved
from divinity.
Already an altar
in motion.

So when love comes—
and it will—
it will have to know:
this body is not a conquest,
not a playground,
not a testing ground
for half-built men
and unfinished intentions.

This body is holy ground.
And only those
who come barefoot,
with reverence,
may enter.

Remember Who You Are

Look in the mirror, love.
No, really—
look.

Not at the flaws you were taught to name,
not at the weight you were told to carry,
not at the lines that map your becoming.

Look deeper.

See the woman who survived
everything meant to break her.
The woman who laughed
with a throat full of ache,
who danced barefoot on floors
built from her own resilience.

Remember the softness
you buried under "strong."
Remember the dreams
you tucked inside your ribs for safekeeping.
Remember the light
that's been waiting,
quiet and patient,
for you to come home to it.

You were never meant
to live small,
to apologize for the glow you carry,
to hand your crown
to people still learning how to lift their own.

So stand up.
Straighten your spine.
Tilt your chin toward the sun.

You are the answered prayer,
the walking miracle,
the living proof
that beauty and power can live in the same skin.

Remember who you are—
not who they told you to be,
not who you became to survive,
but who you were
before the world forgot
how to love women like you.

And when you remember,
when you rise,
when you walk into rooms like you belong—
because you do—
watch the world
try to catch up
to the masterpiece
you were always meant to be.

Unapologetically Unbothered

You Really Tried It

You thought asking would make me eager.
That pressure would turn into passion.
That the woman who once gave freely
could be summoned like a service.

You really tried it.

You forgot who you were dealing with.
Forgot the woman who moved mountains with her silence.
Forgot the woman who blesses with intention—
not obligation.

You really tried it.

You mistook my past love for present access.
Thought you could knock on old doors
and I'd still be standing there,
waiting, wide open.

You really tried it.

But this mouth?
This heart?
This body?
They are no longer moved by hunger or habit.
They respond only to reverence.
Only to the ones who know how to cherish, not chase.

I don't give pleasure from pressure.
I don't give access from assumption.
I don't offer devotion on demand.

You really tried it.

And now you know:
The woman you thought you could summon
has already left the building,
crowned herself Queen,
and locked the door behind her.

Chile, Boo

You used to call
and I'd come running—
heart first,
mouth wide open,
arms stretched like offerings at your altar.
You called it love.
I called it hope.

Chile, boo.
That girl packed her bags and left with her dignity.

You say,
"Remember how good it was?"
As if the echoes of pleasure
could drown out the silence that followed.
As if memory still makes me wet.

Chile, boo.
The only thing you make me feel now is inconvenience.

You keep testing the waters—
dipping your toe into a pool
you let grow stagnant
while I learned to swim in oceans.

Chile, boo.
Your game is shallow, and I float in depth.

You ask for favors with the ease of entitlement—
like I'm still waiting in the wings
for crumbs and callbacks.

Chile, boo.
I'm the whole damn table now, and you ain't got a seat.

You flash that grin,
try to unlock old doors
with expired keys,
expecting to find
the same soft yes
in the same soft places.

Chile, boo.
You didn't realize you got locked out the moment I found the latch.

You confuse my kindness with consent,
my history with permission,
my presence with possibility.

Chile, boo.
I'm only here for the closure you can't give yourself.

I loved you once,
too much, too deep,
too long.

Chile, boo.
Now I love me more.

Healed Eyes Don't Lie

There was a time—
when half-smiles, broken promises,
and *almost* love
made my heart melt.

When bare minimum felt like affection,
and being chosen *eventually*
was enough to call it destiny.

But healing?
Healing changed my sight.
It sharpened my taste.
It detoxed my spirit
from hunger so deep,
I mistook starvation for sweetness.

Now?
Now I look back—
at hands that barely held me,
at eyes that barely saw me,
at mouths that spoke of love
but only knew possession—
and I wonder:

Was I that lonely?
Was I that lost?
Was I that willing to fold myself into crumbs,
just to be tasted?

Healed eyes don't lie.
They don't beg for recognition.
They don't chase what flinches
at the sight of their fullness.

Now?
Now the things that once unraveled me
barely make me blink.
The hands I once craved
look clumsy.
The words I once ached for
sound hollow.

I don't just want love anymore—
I want love that mirrors
the love I now give myself.
I want worship without war,
presence without pretending.

And if you can't meet me in the healed places?
If you still speak in half-truths
and love in half-measures?
I'll bless you from a distance—
with eyes wide open,
and a heart too whole to be fooled.

Because healed eyes don't lie.
They just stop looking back.

She Was the Climate Change

She didn't just enter your life.
She changed the temperature.

You were good before her, sure.
Stable. Comfortable.
But she brought the weather.

She brought the sun through your windows at sunrise,
warmth in your chest when the world felt heavy,
rain when your soul needed cleansing,
thunder when your dreams grew too quiet.

She wasn't just good to you—
she was good for you.

Your laughter got louder.
Your rest got deeper.
Your grind got sharper.
Your days felt lighter,
your nights felt safer.

Her love was infrastructure.
Invisible until it disappeared.
Essential once you had tasted it.

Because without her?

Without her, the air stiffened.
The rooms grew colder.
The blessings slowed their fall.
The edges of your days became sharper again.

Without her, life didn't end—
but it lost its color.

Lost its ease.
Lost the music humming quietly beneath everything you touched.

You see—
men survive without women like her.
Sure.
But they don't thrive.

They live.
But they don't feel alive.

And when they fumble her—
oh, they feel the loss in their marrow.
They feel the drought after the abundance.
The silence after the symphony.

They wander through the ruins of the gardens she once tended,
whispering old jokes to echoes that no longer laugh back.

Because she wasn't just "good company."
She wasn't just "nice to have around."
She was climate change.

She made your ordinary extraordinary.
She made your survival a life worth living.

And when you lost her,
you didn't just lose a woman.
You lost a whole season
you'll never get back.

The Becoming After the Believing

000: The Genesis of Her

Before the world called her broken,
before the bruises,
before the betrayals—
there was only light.

Only possibility.
Only promise.

0.

The beginning before the beginning.
The whispered breath of "You are destined for more."

And now,
after all the shedding,
after all the survival,
after all the soft deaths she endured and rose from—

she returns to that sacred zero.

Not empty.
Infinite.

The Genesis of Her.

The moment where endings bow down
to make room for her rising.

She is not starting over.
She is starting true.

She is not lost.
She is remembered.

And the whole universe leans in to watch her bloom.

Are You Sure?

Sometimes,
even in the arms of love,
the old questions creep back.

Are you sure?
Are you sure you see me?
Are you sure you want this version of me—
the one who's still piecing herself back together in some places?

Are you sure I'm beautiful,
even when I'm not trying?
Even when I'm unguarded, undone, unsure?

Are you sure you're not settling?
Are you sure I'm enough?

And I almost ask.
I almost let the words tumble out,
needy, naked, trembling.

But then I remember.

I remember every tear I caught with my own hands.
Every prayer I whispered through gritted teeth.
Every broken promise I buried without a funeral.
Every scar I turned into scripture.

I remember fussing at my sister
for asking questions that already had their answers
etched into the way he looked at her,
held her,
chose her.

I remember that the woman I am today
is not the woman who needs convincing.

I am not the echo of past rejections.
I am not the bruises they left behind.
I am not the apology for who I've become.

I am the evidence of survival.
I am the answer to prayers prayed generations deep.
I am the blessing wrapped in skin and spirit.

And I deserve this love.

Not because I'm perfect.
Not because I'm easy.
Not because I'm desperate.

But because I am ready.

Ready to receive without shrinking.
Ready to believe without bargaining.
Ready to stand still and let love find me
without running, without doubting, without asking for proof.

He's sure.
I'm sure.
And now, finally—
so is my heart.

She Walks in Power

I walk like I can.

Because I can.
Because this love
made me turn toward the mirror
and see myself—
fully,
fiercely,
finally.

I am no longer asking permission.
I am no longer waiting on a yes
from anyone
but my own mouth.

I stand in the truth
of who I am,
who I can be,
what I can birth,
what I can burn,
what I can build.

There is magic in my bloodstream.
There is alchemy in my bones.
There is thunder
coiled behind my teeth.

And it's spilling over,
crashing into the lives of other women,
igniting their mirrors,
their hands,
their throats,
their hearts.

I was never meant
to keep this power quiet.

I was never meant
to play small
so the world could stay comfortable.

I am the storm.
The shift.
The awakening.

And I am calling you, Sis—
yes, you—
to rise,
to polish your mirror,
to see what the world
has been trying to make you forget.

You are the magic.
You are the answer.
You are the flame
wrapped in thunder and lightning,
and this world
will never
be ready
for what you're about to do.

The Soft Power After Survival

All the heartbreak led me here.

Every lie wrapped in love,
every half-truth whispered
against my skin,
every moment I was mishandled
and made to believe
I was less,
small,
unworthy—
it all led me
here.

For too long,
I ate crumbs
and called it enough.
For too long,
I let others
hold the pen
to my story.

No more.

I have snatched back the pen,
pressed it to the page,
and carved these new chapters
in bold, unshakable letters.

I lit the match,
burned away the bullshit,
turned the ashes to bricks,
and built the altar
of my remembered womanhood.

I am flame
and feast.
I am softness
without surrender.
I am my own
answered prayer.

And the most dangerous thing
about a woman like me
is that I no longer
need to be saved.

I am the hero
and the home.
I am the softness
and the sword.
I am the quiet
and the uprising.

I am
becoming.

In the Presence of Real Love

For the One Who Shows Up

You make laughter feel like prayer.
Like joy is something sacred we get to share
between tickles and inside jokes
and quiet moments that stretch like Sundays.

You see me.
Not the polished version.
Not the one performing strength.
But the real me—
lazy, soft, unfiltered—
and somehow you still look at me like I'm magic.

You listen like my words matter.
You remember the things I forget I said.
You match my energy
without trying to mold me
into something more convenient.

You feed me—
not just with food,
but with attention.
With care.
With warmth.
You make me feel safe and desired.
Not one or the other—
both.

You've made it your job
to find every place joy hides in me—
and bring it to the surface
again and again.

You don't just love me.
You delight in me.

And that?
That's the kind of love
every woman deserves to taste
at least once in her life.

I'm grateful it's you.

Kissed Into Remembering

Every time you kiss me,
I remember.

I remember that I am softness wrapped in fire,
honey wrapped in armor,
the prayer and the promise made flesh.

Your lips on mine are not just affection—
they are invocation.
They summon the woman I fought to become.
They melt away the dust left by hands
that only knew how to grasp,
never how to hold.

When you kiss me,
I forget my fears.
I forget the walls I once thought were necessary.
I forget the silence I used to call strength.

And in their place—
you leave blooming.

You leave a woman unafraid to lavish,
unafraid to give,
unafraid to love so loud
the stars blush and turn away.

Your kiss makes generosity pour from my chest—
not obligation,
but overflow.

Your eyes,
your smile,
your mouth pressed against my existence—

they call forth the best of me.
The sacred of me.
The eternal of me.

You kiss me,
and I remember
that I am worthy of this kind of tenderness.
That I was never asking for too much.
That love,
real love,
is supposed to feel like this:

Soft and certain.
Steady and wild.
Alive.

Every time you kiss me,
I melt.
But not into weakness—
into worship.
Into gratitude.
Into a woman so loved,
she can't help but love in return.

You Speak in a Language I Already Knew

I love you—
but not in the way we're taught to say it.
Not wrapped in performance
or smothered in sound.
I love you in the quiet.
Where breath lingers,
and spirit listens.

You don't just feel good to me.
You feel right.
Like my bones have always known your rhythm,
and my flame recognized your calm
before my mind caught on.

There are moments you finish my thoughts,
and it doesn't startle me—
it settles me.
Like our souls already had the conversation
and we're just here catching up.

You show your love in the in-between.
Not in grand gestures,
but in the way your presence wraps around me
without ever asking me to shrink.

You move like patience,
but your silence is fluent—
your stillness has weight,
and I feel your love
in the way you lean into my fire
without trying to tame it.

I see it when your body softens into mine,
when you rest without guard,

when you reach for me like it's instinct.
You don't speak in declarations.
You speak in comfort.
And I hear every word.

You love me in my language—
the one that listens for energy,
not volume.
The one that recognizes devotion
by how it makes space,
not how it demands attention.

And you encourage my becoming
in a way that doesn't feel like pressure,
but invitation.
You don't chase my light—
you honor it.
You don't compete with my rise—
you root for it.

Because with you,
I don't brace.
I breathe.
I don't fold—
I fall open.
And not once have I had to question
if I'd be caught
or held.

This isn't new.
This is ancient recognition.
A sacred remembering
between flame and thunder.

We are not learning each other—
we're remembering.

And every moment we share
is a map
back to something
we already knew.

What You Pull from Me

They say people don't change.
But I've learned—
people reveal.
Some ignite what's hidden.
Some dim what's divine.
Some love you in a way
that makes you forget how expansive you were meant to be.

Once, I couldn't name a passion.
Not because I didn't have one,
but because I had no breath left to feed the fire.
I was surviving in someone else's weather—
folding my joy to fit their forecast.

But freedom has a sound.
And healing has a rhythm.
And when I stopped living in someone else's shadow,
I finally heard my own voice again.
It was soft at first.
Then steady.
Then undeniable.

And now—
now I move with intention,
create with clarity,
speak with a fullness I didn't know I was allowed to carry.
Not because I've become someone new...
but because I'm no longer being edited.

And isn't it wild...
how some people bring out your brilliance
and others bring out your coping mechanisms?

Some turn your laughter loose,
while others make you forget you ever liked the sound.

I've seen it in others too—
the way love can soften a voice,
lighten a step,
open a person like morning light through a window.

And I wonder...
how much of who we are
is just who we've been allowed to be?

Maybe some of us are whole oceans
who were just waiting
for someone to stop building dams.

So no, you didn't know this version of me.
Because you never made space for her to arrive.
You never knocked on the door of my fullness—
you only admired the quiet hallway.

But she's here now.

Unbothered.
Unbound.
Unapologetic.

This isn't a new me.
This is just the part you never met
because you didn't bring her out.

I Come Undone

I don't fall apart anymore.
I come undone—
on purpose.
With intention.
With hands I trust
and eyes that speak fluency in *me*.

You touch me,
and suddenly I am
not a woman with a name—
but a moment.
A mood.
A memory in the making.
Breathless.
Boundless.
Unfolding like permission with skin on.

I don't melt for just anyone.
But when I do—
I drip in confessions,
slip into vulnerability like lace.
And you?
You wear my unraveling like a gift.
Not a conquest.

You don't tear me down.
You *unwind* me.
Call me out of hiding with your tongue.
Say my name like prayer,
press your hands where I'm most sacred,
and wait—

not to take,
but to *witness*.

I don't give you my body.
I give you the version of me
that doesn't need armor.
The part that moans in truth,
not performance.
The one that doesn't fake anything,
especially not joy.

I come undone
when I feel safe.
When the room holds my softness
without breaking it.
When the moment is full of yes,
and the silence is louder than the act.

So no—
this isn't falling apart.
This is divine release.
This is soul-deep intimacy
that can't be performed,
only *felt*.

I don't break for you.
I bloom.

I come undone—
and somehow,
feel more whole
every time.

Let It Burn

They'll call it crazy.
They'll call it reckless.
They'll say you loved too fast,
too deeply,
too much.

Let them talk.

Your spirit knows better.
It knows the difference between a wildfire that consumes
and a hearth fire that keeps you alive.

It knows the feeling of being met.
Being seen.
Being held in a way that doesn't ask you to shrink,
only to stay.

You feel the fire rise—
not to burn you down,
but to light you up.

You feel the tremble in your bones—
not fear,
but memory.
Not danger,
but home.

So you let it burn.

You let the old doubts turn to smoke.
You let the old walls fall like ash.
You let the love you once thought you had to beg for
wrap you without hesitation.

You are not foolish for trusting your own heart.

You are not reckless for recognizing real things
when they reach for you.

You are not empty.
You are ablaze.

And from now on,
you will not dim,
you will not deny,
you will not doubt
the fire that built you
and the love that finds you.

Let it burn,
beautiful girl.
Let it burn.

Ignited

You don't just love me—
you *ignite* me.

You turn quiet skin into song,
pull breath from places I'd forgotten,
and incite me to poetry
with nothing but your eyes.

You love me from the crown of my head,
where your hands linger like a benediction,
to the soles of my feet,
where you make me feel like no road has ever deserved
me.

You love me in the quiet between words,
in the spaces where I don't have to explain myself.
You love me like a language
you were born knowing,
like you've been fluent in my soul
since before we met.

You don't just touch my body—
you touch the ache I never confessed.
You press your forehead to mine,
and in that small, trembling moment,
I remember what it means
to belong
without bargaining.

And here I am—
all flame,
all chorus,
all yes,

singing a love
I once thought
was only written for other women.

You ignite me.
You incite me.
And I,
I am done
pretending I was ever meant
to live unlit.

What She Walked Away From

She Wasn't the Problem

He didn't leave because she lacked love.
He left because her love was too honest
for a man still hiding from himself.

She didn't push too hard—
she just showed up.
Fully.
Gently.
Without flinching at the places he refused to clean.

And that terrified him.

Because he wasn't ready
to be held without hiding.
To be known without performance.
To be loved
without earning it in pain.

He called her "too much"
because he wasn't enough for himself.
He made her feel loud
because he couldn't hear his own truth.
He kept her close
but never opened the door all the way.

She tried.
Again and again.
Tried to believe that patience was a plan
and presence was enough.
Tried to soften her voice,
make her asks smaller,
carry what he wouldn't even name.

But healing doesn't happen
when one person does all the lifting.

And real love doesn't have to beg
to be met.

She thought if she just loved him louder,
he'd finally believe he was worth it.

But he didn't want light.
He wanted shelter from it.

And so she stopped twisting herself
into smaller shapes.
Stopped confusing pain with passion.
Stopped waiting for someone
to choose her
after abandoning themselves.

She wasn't the problem.
She was just the mirror.
And some people will shatter the glass
before they ever face their reflection.

The Door is Closed

You say you're still madly in love with me.
But tell me—
when did you ever love me
in a way that left me whole?

You reached for my body,
but never rose to meet my spirit.
You called me "wife"
but treated me like a placeholder.
You wanted the title,
not the tending.
The access,
not the effort.

You thought my patience
was your permission.
My softness,
your entitlement.
You mistook survival for devotion
and called it love
because you never learned the difference.

I gave you a thousand chances
to rise,
to reach,
to *see* me—
not just as a woman in your bed,
but as a woman
who deserved to be chosen
every damn day.

But you were busy
folding into smallness,

while I was busy
growing out of it.

And now,
you feel the climate shift?
Baby,
I am the wildfire
that reset the season.

I don't hate you.
I don't wish you harm.
I wish you awakening.
But understand this—
the woman who once made room for your becoming
has burned her own way forward.
And you,
standing in yesterday's ashes,
are not invited to follow.

The door is closed.
The earth has shifted.
And you—
you no longer have the currency
to buy your way back in.

She Set the Fire

There was a time
she thought love had to cut.
That the bruises were proof of passion,
that the silence was a test,
that the chaos was just chemistry
in a tangled disguise.

She learned to live
in the ache between apologies.
She called the shouting
a kind of music.
She called the waiting
a kind of devotion.

But deep inside,
something small and sharp
kept whispering—
no, this is not love.
this is a performance of survival.

She ignored it.
Until she couldn't.

Until the mirror
refused to reflect
the woman she once knew.
Until the pillow
held too many tears
to count as a home.
Until the ache
became too heavy
to wear as jewelry.

So one day—
she set the fire.
Not out of anger,
but out of mercy.

She burned the old story.
She lit the lies.
She torched the need
to be chosen by someone
who only loved
her breaking.

And when the smoke cleared,
she didn't rise
like the phoenix they promised—
she stood,
calm,
whole,
untouched by the ash.

Because healing
isn't always a rebirth.
Sometimes,
it's just walking away
and never
looking
back.

...in closing

*May you rise
from every version of yourself
you once thought you had to become.*

*May you lay down
the armor that never fit,
the silence that never saved,
the guilt that was never yours to carry.*

*May you walk away
from every table
where your voice was too small
and your heart was too loud.*

*May you bless your own name
the way you've blessed everyone else's.*

*May you be soft,
not because you were conquered,
but because you have chosen
to live free.*

*And when the world tries to tell you
to shrink, to harden, to apologize—
may you remember:
you were never broken,
only unfolding.*

Acknowledgements

*To every woman who handed me her story in whispers,
who sat with me in joy, ache, or silence—
this book is as much yours as it is mine.*

*To the women who called me sister,
who let me cry,
laugh,
rage,
and rise in their presence:
thank you for being both mirror and shelter.*

*To the loves that taught me,
to the heartbreaks that broke me open,
to the healing that felt like both fire and balm—
thank you.
You made this becoming necessary.*

*To the version of myself I kept abandoning and
relearning,
this is my promise:
I will never again ask you to shrink
to fit inside someone else's love.*

*To the one who came into my life
like a quiet revolution—
for the laughter, the softness, the steady hands.
For seeing me whole and holding me anyway.
You remind me daily that peace can be a person.*

*And finally,
to the women holding this book in trembling hands,
whispering to themselves, "this is me"—
may you remember:
you were never broken,
only unfolding.*

About the Author

Francesca Tonge is a nurse rediscovering her love of writing and using it as another way to heal. Her poetry speaks to the quiet resilience and tender strength of women on their journey back to themselves. *Unfolding Her* is a reflection of her own becoming and a gift for others on the path.

www.ingramcontent.com/pod-product-compliance
Lightning Source LLC
Chambersburg PA
CBHW050324010526
44119CB00003B/95